T0086371

Hope

and

Healing

Hope

and

Healing

A Collection of Poems

Tom Mueller

HOPE AND HEALING
A COLLECTION OF POEMS

Cover Art by Allen Murphy

iUniverse books may be ordered through booksellers or by contacting:

iUniverse
1663 Liberty Drive
Bloomington, IN 47403
www.iuniverse.com
844-349-9409

ISBN: 978-1-6632-2420-0 (sc)
ISBN: 978-1-6632-2421-7 (e)

Library of Congress Control Number: 2021913711

Print information available on the last page.

iUniverse rev. date: 07/12/2021

For my late mother, whose life, upon her recovery
from alcohol addiction, became a beautiful poem

Contents

Introduction ix

When I Hear a Bird Sing.. 1
Do Not Yield 3
The Rock Chapel 5
First Step 7
Shadow of Light 9
Now 11
Out of the Abyss.. 13
Releasing 15
Hope 17
Times Distant Yet Near 19
Falling Away... 21
Twenty Syllables of Love... 23
Birth and Renewal 25
Circle of Pain... 27
Distant Church Bell 29
Ten Years 31
Each Moment 33
Sitting by a Creek 35
Mountain Place.. 37
Quieting Fear 39
Rapture 41
Hope and Healing 43
Surrender 45
Embrace the Night 47
Triumph with Grace 49
Whisper 51

Acknowledgments.. 53

Introduction

This collection of poems is inspired by three areas of my life experiences. First is working as a volunteer for twelve years at the H. Lee Moffitt Cancer and Research Center in Tampa. I have always been very moved by the courage of those battling cancer and by the commitment of families and caregivers to provide support throughout this battle.

Second is my relationship with my wife, Janet, who is now a twenty-eight-year brain tumor survivor. Despite having lost most of her vision as a result of the tumor, she maintains a very steadfast faith and positive attitude, both of which are very inspirational to me.

Third is my own struggle, not with cancer but with major depressive disorder. It was in the throes of depression that I learned to maintain hope; in emerging from depression I have been able to take steps toward healing. I am very grateful to continue my life's journey, knowing what it means to summon courage and maintain hope while lost in the darkness of despair.

I am hopeful that in reading one or all of these poems, you will come closer to connecting with your own wellspring of hope and, in so doing, continue your own process of healing. Thank you for reading, and may your journey lead you to places that perhaps you thought were not possible to reach.

Tom Mueller

When I Hear a Bird Sing

When I hear a bird sing
early in the morning
or feel the cooling rain
wash over me,

When the wind blows
on a crisp autumn day
or I gaze at the soft colors
of a November sunset,

I sense the sacredness
of each moment
and glimpse that all of life
is evolving in harmony.
I have only to open my eyes
and see.

Do Not Yield

Do not yield
to fear.
Your pain is real,
and healing
requires your strength.

Summon
all your courage;
focus
all your resolve
on healing.

Release
worry and anxiety.
Find
the quiet space within.
Persevere,
and do not yield.

The Rock Chapel

A candle flame
softly glows
inside a small rock chapel
high atop a hill.

It took hours for me to arrive here,
and now time stands still
as I gaze mesmerized
by the burning flame.
I feel a shudder inside,
a wordless voice
that suggests this candle
will burn forever.
I sense that the light
of this candle flame
is my soul burning ever brightly
in timeless wonder.

Remembering Austria
Summer 1985

First Step

That place of darkness
where once no light shone.
Frightened and alone
in the abyss like
drowning, no
breaths to take.
Hope seems so far away.

Then suddenly
the first gasping breath:
Have I reached the surface?
Is that the sun's ray?
The beginning of a life
becoming strong
perhaps for the first time.

Never giving away
the resolve to heal,
the will to live,
the courage to be.
Each new day
a first step
beyond today.

For one of my sisters

Shadow of Light

Sometimes during moments of inner
silence,
I see a small ebony sphere
ringed in gold.

My eyes closed to distractions,
I watch the sphere float
in four-dimensional space.

The sphere suggests that
I empty my mind of thoughts and
expectations
to allow the silence to speak.

Through the keyhole of my mind
I feel my spirit move, freed
from the bindings I place upon myself.

This silent power carries me past darkness,
allowing me to sense that darkness holds
no fear,
that it is only the shadow of light.

Darkness and light,
each within my mind,
each guiding my heart.

Now

Time passing
each day seems
like a moment—
each year
only an hour.

If I try to grasp
time past or
time yet spent,
I lose the time
that is now.
Being present in
the moment,
I find that past and future
dissolve,
along with my angst
over what was
or what is yet
to be.
Embracing each moment
as if it were
a newborn kitten,
listening to it purr,
feeling its furry love,
yet not holding on
when it wants to
slip away.

Out of the Abyss

Wandering
lost
in the darkness.
Wherever I am,
whomever I am with,
I am squeezed in a vise
of despair.

I can't think.
I'm hollow inside.
I want to get out
of wherever I am.
I'm nowhere
except in pain.

But if I can feel
the immensity of
my pain,
I can shatter my fear.
If I can allow
my anger to explode,
I can release my remorse.

Then I can begin
to walk
out of the darkness,
out of the abyss.

Releasing

Releasing the judgments that
tangle my mind;
releasing the self-pity that
burdens my heart;
releasing the fears that
hold me in place;
releasing the pain of that
which has passed;
detaching from all that
binds me;
going inside
to touch
the golden sphere of love.

Hope

Lying awake, frightened.
It's the middle of the night.
The house is quiet
except for the hum
of night noises
and the incessant churning
of my thoughts.

The past weeks
have been difficult,
my strength drained
by the drugs,
my senses dulled,
my spirit challenged.
When will my courage return?
But in the darkness
of this night
I begin to feel warmth inside,
and somewhere
a bright candle burns,
bringing an awareness of healing
and a growing sense of hope.

I vow to continue my fight.
I vow that I will begin to live.
I vow to embrace my soul
and connect with the infinite spirit
of life.

Times Distant Yet Near

The sky is gray
this winter's day,
not the dark mysterious gray
of a nearing thunderstorm
nor the soft contemplative gray
that blankets a forest floor.

It is a mocking gray,
neither dark nor light,
neither loathing nor unkind,
that intrudes upon my tranquility.

I think of times now distant
yet always near,
times of potent anguish
and penetrating gloom,
times of remorse
and crippling fear,
times that would not pass,
leaving me stuck
in the mire
of anger and grief.

But today I smile at the gray
feeling, the gentle peace that harbors
deeply within,
a peace that encircles and nurtures,
a peace born of love
that each day I embrace
and each day I set free.

Falling Away

The crunching sound of
dried leaves under my boots
is deafening in contrast with
the gentle sound of
the wind blowing through
the tall maple trees.

How many layers of
leaves are beneath my feet?
How many seasons have passed?

If I were a leaf,
how would I prepare for
the day when I must wither and
fall away from the mother tree?
Would I think about
being thrown onto a burning pyre
or becoming part of
the moist earth?

Would I hope to
be captured by the wind and
held gently aloft, free to
float to places far away?

Or would I simply
greet my life's end with
a hesitant nod and
then drop quietly away into
the darkness of night?

Twenty Syllables of Love

Gently close
your eyes.
See through
the curtain
of darkness
into the
light of
your heart.

Birth and Renewal

The new growth of springtime
replaces winter's purge,
life dying to new life.
Fragrances abound.

Nature begins its cycle anew:
birth, growth, aging, and death.
Each has a season.
Each has a purpose.
All part of life's plan.
Within my life,
many cycles have passed,
and in time
destructive habits have died
and enriching behaviors have been born.

I deepen my awarenessof my divine nature
when I am patient and accepting,
when I approach others with kindness,
when I give and receive love willingly
and without boastfulness.

The new growth of springtime
offers promise and hope
that from the sacrifice of death
new life is born.

Circle of Pain

Pain does not wait
for morning.
It is not linear and finite
like time.
Pain transcends time.
Pain is a circle that
circumscribes joy.

Distant Church Bell

In the darkness of early morning
I hear the ring
of a distant church bell
echoing through the still air.

No other sounds,
for the birds still slumber
and the crickets
have grown weary.
It occurs to me
how precious silence can be,
gentle spaces wedged between
the calamitous din.

The silence yields to the thought
of how small and alone I can feel,
being slowly squeezed by my pain,
left defenseless in my sorrow.
Then at once I glimpse
the silence as healing,
the aloneness as illusion,
the pain as fleeting,
the sorrow as cleansing.
And in this instant
I glimpse the hope
present in this and every moment.

Ten Years

Ten years have passed
since that pivotal day.
A decade spent
with moments of fear
amid great courage,
with moments of sadness
amid great joy.
Ten years ago
you experienced renewal
not as you would have planned
but as the universe gave to you
to learn patience,
to practice acceptance,
to wonder,
to give thanks.

Ten years after,
how thankful I am
that it was not your time
to quietly pass away.
How thankful I am
to know the strength of your will,
to feel the warmth of your smile,
to receive the depth of your love.
Ten years later
you are a very bright light
to everyone whom you touch.

For Janet

Each Moment

Time waits not
to be grasped.
Each moment is precious;
each moment shall pass.

If I could hold this moment,
what would that moment be?
What achievement would it capture?
What feeling would it sustain?

Time waits not for youth or old age,
not for any hope or any dream.
It simply flows like water
through my open hands.

Sitting by a Creek

Sitting by a creek,
listening to its gentle babble as
it carves its way down the mountain.

My mind runs with the creek,
each syncopated sound
accompanied by a shift in my thoughts.

While none seem to linger,
each leaves a brushstroke
on the canvas of my life.
Many brushstrokes of varying widths
and hues,
some bold and self-assured,
others tentative and doubtful.

Cascading, at times full,
at times shallow
my life flows.

Listening to its gentle babble as
it carves its way
down the mountain.

Mountain Place

I can see the mountains
far in the distance
as I stare across
the barrenness of
empty desert.

I feel the loneliness of
the dry windswept sand,
yet I continue moving forward,
carrying the burden of
my pain.
I know the mountains;
they are cool and serene.
I can follow a creek to
a waterfall and rest
beneath a canopy of trees.

To continue forward,
I must believe in the mountain place
rising high into the sky.
I must believe that
it is not a distant place
but something that is within me now.

Remembering Tucson, Arizona
February 1992

Quieting Fear

Not something to
awaken sadness
or vanquish
the calm of sleep.
The heat that rises
from anxiety
is quenched
by surrendering
to a dream.
Breathing deeply
not of labor
but of faith.
No amplification
of that which is small,
and no fear
of that which is large.

Accepting all
as part of the whole.
Balanced
in quiet slumber.

Rapture

White star
burning a hole through
the moonless sky,
a searing laser point
of light.
Wrapped in
the silk fabric of
the infinite mystery,
my mind leaps,
arching through the
bright hope of
early morning,
when I awaken from
an opaque dream
to the rapture
of your love.

Hope and Healing

No privacy.
My hospital room is
like a staging area.
Sometimes
I don't want to talk
or to listen.
I just want
to be alone
for a few hours.
No vitals taken,
no meals served,
no cheery hellos—
just me
and my thoughts
about hope,
about healing,
about living fully
once again.

Surrender

Sometimes the energies
of my body
are depleted.
Devoured by pain,
my strength seems
to surrender.

The slow movement
of time
brings no respite.
My expectations wane.
I struggle
with futility.
Yet, to surrender
is not to yield;
in surrender
I affirm my resolve
to reach past darkness
to touch the light.

Embrace the Night

What day is this
come to pass?
What light is this
that shines so bright?
What place is this
of yonder lore?
Think now
that all is ripe,
no future yet
to behold.
Let go so tight.
Embrace the night
before the morrow
dawns once more.

Triumph with Grace

Adversity smiles
upon you.
Disguised as a foe,
it makes quick
your strength.

To prevail
is not assured,
for no victory
is foretold.
Fortuitous calamities
stalk like shadows
in the night.
Yet in the end
you will overcome all
that adversity begets,
persevere
with courage and resolve,
triumph
with grace and dignity,
hold high
your prize.

Inspired by Laura B., former two-time
high school cross-country champion

Whisper

The whisper
in my heart
is calming.
Though softly spoken,
it yields strength.
The whisper
in my heart
elicits courage
and gently nurtures
my resolve.
The whisper
in my heart
is in all hearts,
rooted deeply,
transcending time,
giving love,
giving hope,
giving life.

Acknowledgments

Thank you to my wife, Janet, for her comments on these poems, but mostly for her inspiration and ever-abiding love. She is the epitome of strength and courage in the face of one of life's most difficult challenges, and she is a gift to me.

Thank you to my dear friend Allen Murphy, artist extraordinaire and fellow poet, for his faithful support; and his commitment in helping me stagger through the most difficult times in my life. I am also grateful for his drawing on the cover of this book.

Thank you to Alex Murphy, accomplished poet and percussionist and PhD student in mechanical engineering at the Georgia Institute of Technology, whose review and commentary of this book is greatly appreciated.

Thank you to Dr. Xiao Zhang, who genius with acupuncture has been immensely helpful in assisting me to maintain a balanced mind and body. Dr. Zhang is also a poet whose poems are written in English and in her native Chinese.

Thank you to the wonderful staff of iUniverse for their knowledge and expertise in courteously and sincerely helping me to publish this book.

And finally, thank you to all my friends, family, and supporters, past and present, who have smiled upon me and given their heartfelt nod to the publishing of this book.

Printed in the United States
by Baker & Taylor Publisher Services